SUPER KETO SMOOTHIES AND JUICES

Making Ketosis Easy

By Elizabeth Jane

BONUS KETO SWEET EATS SERIES

I am delighted you have chosen my book to help you start or continue on your keto journey. Temptation by sweet treats can knock you off course so, to help you stay on the keto track, I am pleased to offer you three mini ebooks from my 'Keto Sweet Eats Series', completely free of charge! These three mini ebooks cover how to make everything from keto chocolate cake to keto ice cream to keto fat bombs so you don't have to feel like you are missing out, whatever the occasion.

Simply visit the link below to get your free copy of all three mini ebooks...

http://geni.us/smoothiebonus

INTRODUCTION

It may seem strange that by eating 'lots of fat' you can be healthier, but that is the promise and science behind the Low Carb Diet. You can have your (high fat/low carb) cake and eat it too! By sticking to a low carb diet, there are numerous benefits, including:

- Accelerated fat loss
- Lower cholesterol
- Lower blood sugar
- Increased energy and vitality
- Improved mental focus (ketogenic diets were initially used for epilepsy)

Sometimes I am busy and find it difficult to get enough of the right kind of calories. It is easy to grab a sandwich, packet of crisps etc... but not so easy to just grab a quick 'fat fix'. This is when I discovered the power of the smoothie: a quick and easy way to get macros you need.

All of the smoothies contain less than 10g of NET carbs. Most of the carbs come from low GI fruit. I often struggled to get my fix of fruit during the week, and missed all the nutrients that comes from fresh fruit... hence smoothies ticked another box. I have created the smoothies with a variety of ingredients to ensure you get a good mix of vitamins and overall a great balance of good foods.

The guidance for the smoothies is quite simple... stick everything into a blender, blend, then either drink or store for when you need it.

I hope you enjoy the recipes and they help you on your journey to a healthier you.

Introduction
Recipe Notes
SMOOTHIES

8
FRUIT

Raspberry Cream Shake **8**

Blueberry Almond Smoothie **9**

Berry Green Smoothie **10**

Strawberry Cheesecake Smoothie **11**

Chocolate-Covered Strawberry Protein Shake

12

Pink Power Smoothie **13**

Strawberry Chia Milkshake **14**

Tropical Raspberry Smoothie

15

Raspberry Almond Smoothie **16**

Avocado Fat-Burning Smoothie **17**

Green Superfood Smoothie **18**

Gingered Plum Smoothie **19**

20
NON-FRUIT

Mocha Shake **21**

Super Green Smoothie **22**

Nutty Fat Bomb Smoothie

23

Chocolate Peanut Butter Shake **24**

Cinnamon Roll Smoothie **25**

Minty Keto Milkshake **26**

Faux Chocolate Frosty **27**

Coconut Mocha Frappe **28**

Coconut Avocado Smoothie **29**

Red Velvet Smoothie

30

31
JUICES

Super Pear Juice **32**

Ginger Grapefruit Green Juice **33**

Tropical Kiwi Juice

Veggie-Packed Green Juice **35**

Cucumber Lemonade **36**

Pineapple Green Juice **37**

Pear Limeade **38**

Zesty Zucchini Juice **39**

RECIPE *NOTES*

There is not a one-size-fits-all recipe, everyone has different tastes, some have allergies and not everyone will be able to get all of the ingredients. Consider the recipes as a guideline to which you can then customize to your own taste or to what you have in the house.

- Love coconut? Try coconut milk instead of almond milk.
- Do not like strawberries? Try blueberries.

Only you know what your preferences are, so have some fun with it and play around with different ingredients and recipes.

The book is divided into smoothies and juices. What is the difference? Smoothies will have a thicker consistency and will usually involve milk or ice to thicken them. The smoothies are furthered divided into fruit vs non-fruit. The fruit variants will have a slightly higher NET carb count (but still low). Do not shy away from these though, fruits contain a whole range of nutrients that are great for your overall health.

And lastly, if you would be kind enough to leave an honest review it would be most appreciated. Please visit the link below.

http://www.amazon.com/product-reviews/B01F5G1FT8

Once again, thank you for downloading and good luck.

Elizabeth Jane

smoothie- fruit

RASPBERRY
CREAM SHAKE
SERVES: 1

INGREDIENTS
⅔ cup raspberries, fresh or frozen
¼ cup heavy whipping cream
¼ cup coconut cream
½ cup water
1 tablespoon coconut oil
½ teaspoon vanilla extract
½ cup ice
3-4 drops liquid stevia *(optional)*

INSTRUCTIONS
1. Place all ingredients, except for the optional stevia, into a blender and blend until smooth and creamy.

2. Taste and sweeten with liquid stevia, if desired. Blend.

3. Enjoy!

NUTRITION FACTS (PER SERVING)
Total Carbs: 14g   Fiber: 7g   Net Carbs: 7g   Total Fat: 40g   Protein: 3g   Calories: 401

BLUEBERRY
ALMOND SMOOTHIE
SERVES: 1

INGREDIENTS
¼ cup frozen blueberries
6 unsalted almonds
1 cup unsweetened almond milk
2 ounces heavy whipping cream
½ scoop vanilla protein powder
1 teaspoon sugar-free sweetener

OPTIONAL GARNISH
Fresh blueberries and/or toasted almond slices

INSTRUCTIONS
1. Place all ingredients, except for the optional garnish, into a blender and blend until smooth.

2. You may need to add a bit of water to achieve desired consistency.

3. Top with fresh blueberries and/or toasted almond slices, if desired.

NUTRITION FACTS (PER SERVING)
Total Carbs: 13g   Fiber: 3g   Net Carbs: 10g   Total Fat: 31g   Protein: 25g   Calories: 406

Berry
GREEN SMOOTHIE
SERVES: 1

INGREDIENTS
¼ cup frozen blueberries
1 cup fresh spinach
½ cup plain Greek yogurt
½ cup unsweetened almond milk
1 cup ice

INSTRUCTIONS
1. Place all of the ingredients except for the ice into your blender and blend until smooth.

2. Add the ice, and blend for another minute until the ice is crushed. Additional almond milk may be needed to achieve desired consistency.

3. Serve right away.

NUTRITION FACTS (PER SERVING)
Total Carbs: 12g   Fiber: 2g   Net Carbs: 10g   Total Fat: 2g   Protein: 15g   Calories: 128

STRAWBERRY
CHEESECAKE SMOOTHIE
SERVES: 1

INGREDIENTS
½ cup frozen strawberries
½ cup reduced-fat cottage cheese
1 cup unsweetened almond milk
1 teaspoon vanilla extract
1 teaspoon stevia
1 cup ice

OPTIONAL GARNISH
Fresh strawberries

INSTRUCTIONS
1. Place all of the ingredients except for the ice into your blender and blend until smooth.

2. Add the ice, and blend for another minute until the ice is crushed.

3. Garnish with fresh strawberry, if desired, and serve immediately.

NUTRITION FACTS (PER SERVING)
Total Carbs: 12g   Fiber: 2g   Net Carbs: 2g   Total Fat: 5g   Protein: 16g   Calories: 161

CHOCOLATE-COVERED
STRAWBERRY PROTEIN SHAKE
SERVES: 1

INGREDIENTS
1 cup frozen strawberries
1 scoop chocolate protein powder
2 tablespoons cocoa powder
¼ cup raw almonds
1 tablespoon coconut oil
1 tablespoon hemp seeds
2 cups unsweetened almond milk

OPTIONAL GARNISH
Cacao nibs

INSTRUCTIONS
1. Place all ingredients into your blender and blend on high until smooth and creamy.

2. Pour into 2 glasses and garnish with cacao nibs, if desired.

3. Serve and enjoy!

NUTRITION FACTS (PER SERVING)
Total Carbs: 16g   Fiber: 6g   Net Carbs: 10g   Total Fat: 20g   Protein: 17g   Calories: 288

PINK
POWER SMOOTHIE
SERVES: 2

INGREDIENTS
1 cup frozen strawberries

½ avocado

2 celery stalks, roughly chopped

1 ½ cups coconut water

Juice of 1 lemon

1 tablespoon coconut oil

4 ice cubes

OPTIONAL GARNISH
Fresh strawberries

INSTRUCTIONS
1. Place all of the ingredients into a blender and blend on high until smooth and creamy.

2. Divide between two glasses, garnish with fresh strawberry, if desired, and serve.

NUTRITION FACTS (PER SERVING)
Total Carbs: 147g   Fiber: 8g   Net Carbs: 9g   Total Fat: 17g   Protein: 3g   Calories: 235

STRAWBERRY
CHIA MILKSHAKE
SERVES: 1

INGREDIENTS

½ cup frozen strawberries
1 tablespoon chia seeds
¼ cup heavy whipping cream
¾ cup unsweetened almond milk
1 tablespoon coconut oil
½ teaspoon vanilla extract

OPTIONAL GARNISH

Fresh strawberries

INSTRUCTIONS

1. Place all ingredients into a blender and pulse until ingredients are combined.

2. Blend on high for 30-60 seconds.

3. Garnish with a fresh strawberry, if desired, and enjoy!

NUTRITION FACTS (PER SERVING)
Total Carbs: 14g   Fiber: 7g   Net Carbs: 7g   Total Fat: 30g   Protein: 4g   Calories: 336

TROPICAL
RASPBERRY SMOOTHIE
SERVES: 1

INGREDIENTS
1 cup of frozen raspberries
¼ cup silken organic tofu
½ cup unsweetened coconut milk
1 teaspoon sugar-free sweetener
1 cup ice

OPTIONAL GARNISH
Fresh mint leaves

INSTRUCTIONS
1. Place all of the ingredients into the blender except for the ice and the stevia. Blend until smooth.

2. Add in the ice and stevia and blend for another minute.

3. Taste and if needed, adjust the sweetness by adding another pinch of stevia.

NUTRITION FACTS (PER SERVING)
Total Carbs: 21g   Fiber: 11g   Net Carbs: 10g   Total Fat: 32g   Protein: 8g   Calories: 381

RASPBERRY
ALMOND SMOOTHIE
SERVES: 1

INGREDIENTS
½ cup frozen raspberries
2 tablespoons unsalted almonds
½ cup unsweetened almond milk
1 scoop vanilla protein powder

OPTIONAL GARNISH
Toasted almond slices

INSTRUCTIONS
1. Place all of the ingredients, except the optional garnish, into your blender and blend until smooth.

2. Additional almond milk may be needed to reach desired consistency.

3. Garnish with toasted almond slices, if desired, and serve.

NUTRITION FACTS (PER SERVING)
Total Carbs: 20g   Fiber: 9g   Net Carbs: 11g   Total Fat: 12g   Protein: 26g   Calories: 303

Avocado
FAT-BURNING CREAM SHAKE
SERVES: 1

INGREDIENTS
½ of an avocado
½ kiwi fruit
1 tablespoon fresh lime juice
1 tablespoon chopped chives
½ cup unsweetened almond milk
1 tablespoon heavy cream
½ cup ice
Pinch of sea salt

INSTRUCTIONS
1. Place all of the ingredients except for the ice into your blender and blend until smooth.

2. Add the ice and blend until the ice is crushed.

3. Serve and enjoy!

NUTRITION FACTS (PER SERVING)
Total Carbs: 10g   Fiber: 5g   Net Carbs: 5g   Total Fat: 17g   Protein: 2g   Calories: 189

Green
SUPERFOOD SMOOTHIE
SERVES: 1

INGREDIENTS

1 cup fresh spinach
¼ cup frozen pineapple
½ an avocado
1 tablespoon fresh parsley
¼ teaspoon freshly grated ginger
1 cup water
Handful of ice

INSTRUCTIONS

1. Place all of the ingredients except for the ice into your blender and blend until smooth.

2. Add in the ice, and blend for another minute until the ice is crushed.

3. Serve right away.

NUTRITION FACTS (PER SERVING)
Total Carbs: 13g   Fiber: 6g   Net Carbs: 7g   Total Fat: 10g   Protein: 3g   Calories: 138

Gingered
PLUM SMOOTHIE
SERVES: 2

INGREDIENTS

1 cup frozen plum pieces

½ cup chopped raw beet

1 small piece fresh ginger (about ½')

½ cup canned coconut milk

1 cup water

1 tablespoon almond butter

1 tablespoon coconut oil

¼ teaspoon cinnamon

½ cup ice

INSTRUCTIONS

1. Place all ingredients into your blender and blend until smooth and creamy.

2. Serve immediately or store in the fridge for later.

NUTRITION FACTS (PER SERVING)

Total Carbs: 11g   Fiber: 3g   Net Carbs: 8g   Total Fat: 26g   Protein: 6g   Calories: 281

Mocha
SHAKE
SERVES: 1

INGREDIENTS
2 cups unsweetened almond milk

2 teaspoons instant coffee granules

1 tablespoon cocoa powder

½ cup full-fat plain yogurt

½ teaspoon vanilla extract

1 teaspoon sugar-free sweetener

OPTIONAL GARNISH
Coconut flakes

INSTRUCTIONS
1. Place all ingredients into a shallow, freezer-safe bowl and mix well.

2. Place in the freezer and scrape the mixture with a fork once an hour for 4-5 hours.

3. Once the mixture is frozen, set on the counter to soften a bit.

4. Place the mixture in your blender and blend until smooth and creamy.

5. Top with coconut flakes, if desired, and serve.

NUTRITION FACTS (PER SERVING)

Total Carbs: 15g   Fiber: 4g   Net Carbs: 11g   Total Fat: 9g   Protein: 10g   Calories: 179

Super
GREEN SMOOTHIE
SERVES: 1

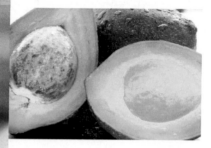

INGREDIENTS
1 cup baby spinach

½ medium avocado

1 cup unsweetened almond milk

1 tablespoon almond butter

1 tablespoon coconut oil

1 teaspoon sugar-free sweetener

5 ice cubes

INSTRUCTIONS
1. Place all ingredients into your blender and blend on high for 30-60 seconds, until smooth and creamy.

2. If mixture is too thick, add a bit more almond milk and blend to desired consistency.

3. Serve.

NUTRITION FACTS (PER SERVING)

Total Carbs: 10g   Fiber: 4g   Net Carbs: 6g   Total Fat:26g   Protein: 6g   Calories: 311

Nutty
FAT BOMB SMOOTHIE
SERVES: 2

INGREDIENTS

1 cup canned coconut milk
1 cup unsweetened almond milk
2 tablespoons coconut oil
2 tablespoons peanut butter
1 teaspoon sugar-free sweetener
½ teaspoon vanilla extract
½ teaspoon cinnamon
1 cup ice

INSTRUCTIONS

1. Starting with the ice, add all ingredients into a blender.

2. Blend until smooth.

3. Can be enjoyed immediately or stored in the fridge for later use, though you may have to give a good stir to mix any ingredients that have settled.

NUTRITION FACTS (PER SERVING)
Total Carbs: 11g   Fiber: 4g   Net Carbs: 7g   Total Fat: 52g   Protein: 7g   Calories: 507

CHOCOLATE PEANUT
BUTTER SHAKE
SERVES: 1

INGREDIENTS
1 tablespoon cocoa powder
1 scoop chocolate protein powder
1 tablespoon peanut butter
1 cup unsweetened almond milk
1 cup ice

INSTRUCTIONS
1. Place all of the ingredients except for the ice into your blender and blend until smooth.

2. Add in the ice, and blend for another minute until the ice is crushed.

3. Serve right away.

NUTRITION FACTS (PER SERVING)
Total Carbs: 12g   Fiber: 4g   Net Carbs: 8g   Total Fat: 14g   Protein: 28g   Calories: 266

CINNAMON
ROLL SMOOTHIE
SERVES: 2

INGREDIENTS
2 cups unsweetened almond milk

½ cup plain yogurt

1 scoop vanilla protein powder

1 teaspoon cinnamon

½ teaspoon vanilla extract

1 teaspoon ground flax seeds

1 teaspoon sugar-free sweetener

1 cup ice

INSTRUCTIONS
1. Place all of the ingredients except the ice into your blender and blend until smooth.

2. Add the ice and blend for another minute until the ice is crushed.

3. Garnish with a sprinkle of cinnamon and serve immediately.

NUTRITION FACTS (PER SERVING)
Total Carbs: 9g   Fiber: 2g   Net Carbs: 7g   Total Fat: 6g   Protein: 16g   Calories: 154

KETO MILKSHAKE

SERVES: 1

INGREDIENTS

1 cup fresh spinach
½ teaspoon peppermint extract
½ an avocado
1 scoop vanilla protein powder
1 cup unsweetened almond milk
8-10 drops liquid stevia, to taste
1 cup ice

INSTRUCTIONS

1. Place the avocado, spinach, protein powder, and milk in a blender and blend until smooth.

2. Add the liquid stevia, peppermint extract, and ice. Blend until smooth.

3. Taste and add additional stevia or peppermint, if desired.

4. Serve and enjoy!

NUTRITION FACTS (PER SERVING)

Total Carbs: 15g   Fiber: 8g   Net Carbs: 7g   Total Fat: 25g   Protein: 26g   Calories: 372

Faux
CHOCOLATE FROSTY
SERVES: 1

INGREDIENTS
1 cup unsweetened almond milk
1 tablespoon cocoa powder
1 scoop chocolate protein powder
2 pitted medjool dates
¼ teaspoon xanthan gum
1 cup ice

INSTRUCTIONS
1. Place all of the ingredients, minus the ice and dates, into your blender and blend until smooth.

2. Add in the ice and dates and blend for another minute until the ice is crushed.

3. Serve right away.

NUTRITION FACTS (PER SERVING)
Total Carbs: 15g   Fiber:4g   Net Carbs: 11g   Total Fat: 6g   Protein: 24g   Calories: 195

Coconut
MOCHA FRAPPE
SERVES: 1

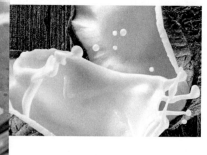

INGREDIENTS
½ cup canned coconut milk
½ cup unsweetened almond milk
2 tablespoons strong black coffee, chilled
1 tablespoon cocoa powder
1 teaspoon sugar-free sweetener
1 cup ice

OPTIONAL GARNISH
1 tablespoon unsweetened, shredded coconut

INSTRUCTIONS
1. Place all of the ingredients except the shredded coconut into your blender and blend until smooth.

2. Top with shredded coconut and serve.

NUTRITION FACTS (PER SERVING)
Total Carbs: 11g   Fiber: 5g   Net Carbs: 6g   Total Fat: 32g   Protein: 4g   Calories: 326

Coconut
AVOCADO SMOOTHIE
SERVES: 1

INGREDIENTS
¼ cup canned coconut milk
½ an avocado
½ cup unsweetened almond milk
1 teaspoon pure vanilla extract
1 teaspoon sugar-free sweetener
1 cup ice

INSTRUCTIONS
1. Place all of the ingredients except the ice into your blender and blend until smooth.

2. Add in the ice, and blend for another minute until the ice is crushed.

3. Serve right away.

NUTRITION FACTS (PER SERVING)
Total Carbs: 13g   Fiber: 9g   Net Carbs: 4g   Total Fat: 36g   Protein: 4g   Calories: 363

RED
VELVET SMOOTHIE
SERVES: 1

INGREDIENTS
½ a beet
½ an avocado
1 tablespoon cocoa powder
1 cup unsweetened almond milk
1 teaspoon sugar-free sweetener
1 cup ice

INSTRUCTIONS
1. Place all of the ingredients except the ice into your blender and blend until smooth.

2. Add in the ice, and blend for another minute until the ice is crushed.

3. Serve right away.

NUTRITION FACTS (PER SERVING)
Total Carbs: 18g   Fiber: 8g   Net Carbs:10g   Total Fat: 13g   Protein: 4g   Calories: 195

juices

Super
PEAR JUICE
SERVES: 1

INGREDIENTS
½ a green pear
1 cup baby spinach
½ an avocado
1 handful of fresh basil
1 cup water

INSTRUCTIONS
1. Place all of the ingredients into your blender and blend until smooth.

2. Additional water may be needed to reach desired consistency.

3. Serve right away.

NUTRITION FACTS (PER SERVING)
Total Carbs: 18g   Fiber: 8g   Net Carbs: 10g   Total Fat: 10g   Protein: 3g   Calories: 167

GINGER
GRAPEFRUIT GREEN JUICE
SERVES: 1

INGREDIENTS
½ a peeled grapefruit
1 small chunk fresh ginger
1 cup fresh spinach
1 handful fresh parsley
1 cup water
1 cup ice

INSTRUCTIONS
1. Place all of the ingredients except the ice into your blender and blend until smooth.

2. Add the ice and blend for another minute until the ice is crushed.

NUTRITION FACTS (PER SERVING)
Total Carbs: 11g   Fiber: 2g   Net Carbs: 9g   Total Fat: 0g   Protein: 2g   Calories: 48

TROPICAL
KIWI JUICE
SERVES: 1

INGREDIENTS

1 peeled kiwi
1 cup coconut water
½ an avocado
1 cup baby spinach
1 handful fresh mint leaves
1 cup ice

INSTRUCTIONS

1. Place all of the ingredients except the ice into your blender and blend until smooth.

2. Add in the ice and blend for another minute until the ice is crushed.

NUTRITION FACTS (PER SERVING)

Total Carbs: 21g   Fiber: 10g   Net Carbs: 11g   Total Fat: 20g   Protein: 4g   Calories: 258

VEGGIE-PACKED
GREEN JUICE
SERVES: 1

INGREDIENTS
4 large kale leaves
3 celery stalks
1 medium cucumber
2 lemons (peeled)
Handful fresh parsley

INSTRUCTIONS
1. Place all of the ingredients through a juicer, and enjoy right away.

NUTRITION FACTS (PER SERVING)
Total Carbs: 18g   Fiber: 8g   Net Carbs: 10g   Total Fat: 1g   Protein:6g   Calories: 128

Cucumber
LEMONADE
SERVES: 1

INGREDIENTS
2 cucumbers
4 celery stalks
2 lemons *(peeled)*

INSTRUCTIONS
1. Run all of the ingredients through a juicer, and enjoy right away.

NUTRITION FACTS (PER SERVING)
Total Carbs: 19g   Fiber: 9g   Net Carbs: 10g   Total Fat: 1g   Protein: 5g   Calories: 108

PINEAPPLE
GREEN JUICE
SERVES: 1

INGREDIENTS

¼ cup pineapple cubes

1 cucumber

2 celery stalks

½ a green apple

3 large romaine leaves

1 small nub fresh ginger, grated

INSTRUCTIONS

1. Place all of the ingredients through a juicer, and chill for 30 minutes before serving.

NUTRITION FACTS (PER SERVING)
Total Carbs: 12g   Fiber: 4g   Net Carbs: 8g   Total Fat: 1g   Protein: 2g   Calories:58

*P*EAR
LIMEADE
SERVES: 1

INGREDIENTS
½ a green pear
1 lime *(peeled)*
2 celery stalks
4 large kale leaves
1 teaspoon sugar-free sweetener

INSTRUCTIONS
1. Place all of the ingredients except the stevia though a juicer, and pour the juice into a glass.

2. Add in the stevia, and stir until dissolved.

3. Enjoy right away.

NUTRITION FACTS (PER SERVING)
Total Carbs: 14g   Fiber: 4g   Net Carbs: 10g   Total Fat: 0g   Protein: 2g   Calories: 70

Zesty
ZUCCHINI JUICE

SERVES: 1

INGREDIENTS

1 medium zucchini

1 cup baby spinach

½ a cucumber

1 nub fresh ginger root, grated

½ cup fresh mint leaves

INSTRUCTIONS

1. Place all of the ingredients through a juicer, and enjoy right away.

NUTRITION FACTS (PER SERVING)
Total Carbs: 11g   Fiber: 4g   Net Carbs: 8g   Total Fat: 1g   Protein: 3g   Calories: 52